LOOKING AT
PREHISTORY

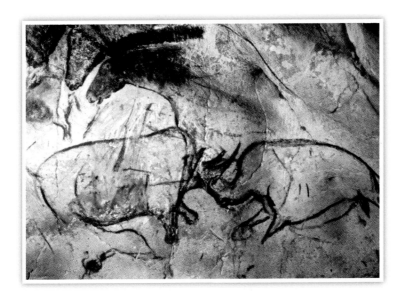

by Ellen B. Cutler

Editorial Offices: Glenview, Illinois • Parsippany, New Jersey • New York, New York

Sales Offices: Needham, Massachusetts • Duluth, Georgia • Glenview, Illinois
Coppell, Texas • Sacramento, California • Mesa, Arizona

The story of the past is told through words and objects.

Talking About the Past

History is the story of things that took place in the past. It tells about the rise and fall of kingdoms, discoveries in science, artistic achievements, and religious beliefs. History is made by people who are famous and by people whose names are no longer known. History is the written record of human **culture**. The documents of history include codes of law, newspaper accounts, personal journals, and business records.

Prehistory is the period of human culture that came before the invention of writing. History is about five thousand years old—but prehistory is much, much older.

Prehistory and Culture

In **anthropology** the word *culture* refers to the shared experiences of a group of people. These shared experiences include both beliefs and learned knowledge.

Beliefs are the ideas and attitudes that influence lives. Social attitudes are beliefs. Social beliefs may cause people to treat some members of a family or a village differently from others.

Learned knowledge is the set of skills that people need to live. Prehistoric people knew how to use fire, make tools, and care for sick or injured individuals. As learned knowledge is handed down from one generation to the next, it is also improved.

Finding, growing, and preparing food are all forms of knowledge.

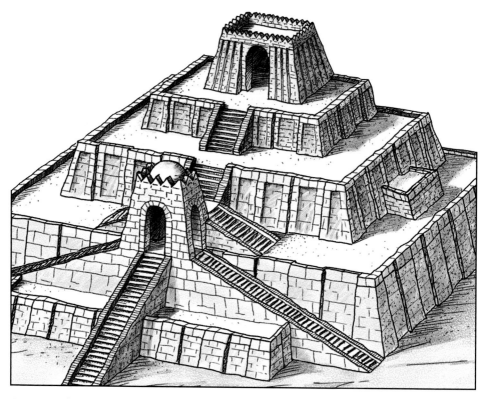

Some prehistoric cities had stone buildings and large temples.

The Beginning and End of Prehistory

Anthropologists, or people who study anthropology, agree that human culture is extremely old. They do not agree, however, on when prehistory began.

Some anthropologists say prehistory started about 2 million years ago when our ancestors began to use tools. Still others say that prehistory started about 100,000 years ago when the first modern human beings appeared.

In general, anthropologists agree that prehistory ended with the invention of written language. Writing was invented, however, at different times in different places. Writing was invented in Egypt and in what is now Iraq about five thousand years ago. Ancient China had a writing system about four thousand years ago. The Aztecs, who lived in Mexico seven hundred years ago, never developed a written language, but they did use a system of simple pictures to keep records.

Prehistory and The Age of Stone

Prehistory is divided into three ages: the Stone Age, the Bronze Age, and the Iron Age. Many scientists disagree as to when each of these ages ended and the next began. What they do agree on is that our prehistory took place almost entirely in the Stone Age.

Early Stone Age peoples were **nomads** who traveled from place to place with the seasons. They collected fruits and nuts and hunted animals. They made tools from things that were easily carried, such as stone, wood, bones, and shells. Late Stone Age cultures discovered **agriculture**. People in these cultures raised cows, horses, goats, and dogs. They grew grains and other plants. At the end of the Stone Age, people settled in villages. Some of the villages grew into cities.

Stone points show that early peoples made tools.

A bronze axe is an example of an early tool.

Metal **technology** marked the end of the Stone Age. At the end of the Stone Age, people learned to heat copper ore to get copper metal. In the Bronze Age they melted copper and tin together to create a harder metal called bronze.

The Iron Age followed the Bronze Age. The Iron Age began about 3,000 years ago. Iron is a stronger metal than bronze, but it is more difficult to work with. Iron tools and weapons were stronger than bronze items and lasted longer.

Moving from One Age to the Next

Knowledge of metal technology often passed from one culture to another. Some peoples were introduced to iron without ever having learned about bronze. Some Stone Age cultures survived so long that they jumped directly into the modern era when they came into contact with European explorers.

A Time Line of Prehistory

The break in the time line means that a part of the time line has been left out. In this case the years between 3 million years ago and 100,000 years ago have been left out of the time line.

Progress During the Stone Age

The Stone Age lasted about 2.5 million years. During the Stone Age, humans spread from the African continent throughout Europe, Asia, and North and South America. They became skilled at making stone tools and also produced many kinds of art, including carved animal figures, cave paintings, and decorated pottery.

Fire was important to prehistoric cultures.

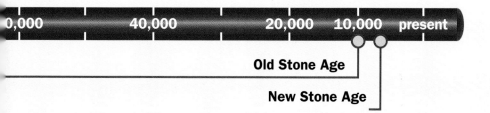

| 0,000 | 40,000 | 20,000 | 10,000 | present |

Old Stone Age

New Stone Age

Using Fire

Perhaps the most important "tool" in prehistory was fire. At first early humans may have taken advantage of small fires caused by lightning. They later figured out how to control these fires and keep them burning. Finally they learned how to start fires themselves. Our ancestors were warming themselves with fire about 450,000 years ago.

Fire kept people warm in cold weather. It protected them from attacks by wild animals. Cooking made food taste better. Meat dried in the smoke did not spoil. A crackling fire would have encouraged people to gather together for warmth, safety, and company. Small fires made it possible to work at night and in dark caves.

This knife with a stone blade and a woven pouch were probably used around the New Stone Age.

The Things They Left Behind

Early Tools

Archaeologists study prehistoric cultures through the **artifacts** they left behind. The oldest artifacts are made from stone.

The first tools were axes, scrapers, and knives. They were made from large pieces of rock that had been broken to produce a sharp edge. After a while Stone Age peoples learned to flake thin pieces from large rocks. These flaked tools had sharp edges and points. They could be attached to sticks or long bones to make arrows and spears for hunting or scythes for cutting grasses and grains.

Stone Age peoples shaped tools from stone, bone, and antler. A variety of points, including spearheads, awls for poking holes in skins, and sewing needles, were made from bone, antler, and ivory.

Carved Objects and Personal Ornaments

The oldest prehistoric works of art were small, portable carvings, such as animal and human figures. Personal ornaments made from ivory, shells, and animal teeth were also common. This made sense for nomads, who were always on the move. Stone Age artists also decorated weapons and other tools.

Did these works of art have a purpose or a special meaning? Could ivory beads, for instance, show that the wearer was an important person? Perhaps an animal figure served as a good-luck charm. There is no way to know for sure.

In addition to paintings, prehistoric people made fine rock carvings.

Paintings and Wall Decorations

Some prehistoric artists were painters who decorated caves and stone cliffs with patterns and pictures. These artists made red, yellow, and brown paints with minerals they dug from the ground. They made black paint from burned bones and wood.

First they ground colors into powder. Then they mixed the colors with water or animal fat. They dabbed this paint on stone with their fingers or with twigs, or used brushes made from animal hair. They also blew dry, powdered color onto the cave walls through hollow bones.

The paintings show a variety of animals, such as wild cattle, horses, lions, deer, woolly mammoths, rhinoceros, and goats. Human figures are rare, but the outlines or prints of human hands are common. Patterns of dots, lines, and spirals decorate some of the caves.

Why did they paint in caves?

The purpose and meaning of these paintings are a mystery. The caves would not have been good homes. They are dark, damp, and hard to get to. Pictures are often high up on walls and very hard to see.

Many people think that the pictures were painted to help the hunters. Prehistoric people hunted many kinds of animals. Other animals appear in the paintings, such as the rhinoceros, but they were not usually hunted for food. The cave paintings at Chauvet, France, show images of rhinoceros fighting with each other.

Perhaps some animals in the paintings represented spirits that Stone Age peoples feared or worshipped. Perhaps the caves were used for religious ceremonies.

Some scholars share the idea that the cave paintings are records to help people remember important ideas and events. When looked at from this point of view, cave paintings are like written records.

This cave painting in Chauvet, France, shows images of horses and rhinoceros.

Who Made It . . . and When?

Archaeologists have to decide when an artifact was made. In order to determine this, it is important to know exactly where an object was found.

Doing the Dig

The first step in studying artifacts is to collect them. The excavation site where archaeologists find objects is called a dig. Each dig is set up so that archaeologists can record exactly where each object was found.

The ground is made up of layers of dirt, stone, and other material. The first clue about the age of an artifact is the age of the layer of earth where it was found.

Archaeologists at a dig work carefully with the artifacts they find.

At the dig, archaeologists make a map of the area. Then they divide it into small sections called units. Each unit has to be searched slowly and carefully.

While some dirt can be removed with shovels and machines, most of it is cleared away with brushes and tiny tools. Workers are careful not to break or scratch precious artifacts.

How old is really old?

Carbon dating is another way to determine how old an artifact is. All living things contain the element carbon. One kind of carbon is called carbon 14, or C14. As long as a plant or animal is alive, it has C14 inside it. When it dies, the C14 starts to disappear. Scientists know that it takes about fifty thousand years for C14 to disappear from a dead plant or animal. If the C14 is all gone, then the object is at least fifty thousand years old. Carbon dating cannot be used on stone, but it can be used on paint or animal blood that is stuck to the stone.

If a cave painting, for instance, has black paint made from burnt wood or bone, a scientist can measure the amount of C14 in the paint. This is how archaeologists decide how old a cave painting might be.

15

Glossary

agriculture the practice of raising plants or animals for human use

anthropology the study of how people have developed and live in cultural groups

archaeologist a scientist who uncovers evidence, or proof, from the past

artifact an object made by people long ago

carbon dating a method of estimating the age of an animal or a plant after it has died

culture the way in which individuals and groups react with their environment, including their technology, customs, beliefs, and art

nomad a person who travels from place to place without a permanent home

prehistory the long period of time before people developed systems of writing and written language

technology the way in which humans produce the items they use

Write to It!

Suppose that you are an archaeologist. What do you think would be the most important kind of artifact that you could find? Write one or two paragraphs describing your artifact and why you think it would be important.

Write your paragraphs on a separate sheet of paper.

Fascinating Facts

- Some Stone Age peoples built huts out of bones, tusks, and hides of woolly mammoths.

- The Dani people of Irian Jaya, on the island of New Guinea, are believed to be the longest surviving Stone Age peoples. European explorers discovered their culture in 1920.

- Some archaeologists believe that the first peoples in North America might not have come across the Bering Sea from Asia on an ice bridge. Artifacts found in Pennsylvania suggest that some groups may have paddled large canoes across the Atlantic Ocean from southwest France.

Genre	Comprehension Skill	Text Features
Nonfiction	Sequence	• Time Line • Captions

Scott Foresman Social Studies

scottforesman.com

ISBN 0-328-14921-7

9 780328 149216

90000

BUILDINGS IN
GREECE AND ROME

BY TAMMY ZAMBO

The ancient Greeks and Romans possessed great skill in designing and building temples and other structures. These structures affected the way Greeks and Romans lived, and the way they lived affected the structures they built. In this book you will read about these structures and their importance in people's lives.

Vocabulary

democracy

architecture

agora

innovation

emperor

gladiator

ISBN: 0-328-14930-6